Dr. Deirdre Avant
The Enemy Within

2020 © Copyright by Deirdre Avant. All rights reserved. This book or any portion thereof may not be reproduced or used in any manner whatsoever without the express written permission of the publisher except for the use of brief quotations in a book review. Printed in the United States of America.

First Printing, 2020

ISBN: 978-0-578-69666-9

The Complete Jewish Bible was copyrighted in 1998 by David H. Stern and is published by Jewish New Testament Publications, Inc. (All rights reserved. Used by permission)

Publishers
Autore
Wilmington, DE 19850
www.mioautore.com

Table of Contents

The Enemy Within

1. Introduction
2. Anger
3. Low Self-Esteem
4. Procrastination
5. Self-Doubt
6. Trust issues
7. Fear of Failure
8. Fear of Success
9. The Final Frontier

INTRODUCTION

In life we are exposed to many things from childhood on up. These experiences leave impressions on our minds and create strongholds that sometimes takes us years to get free from. Bondage and oppression can come in many forms. Some forms are physical like, illnesses brought on by how we think because of these life experiences. Some are mental but are just as bad as physical bondage. In this book we will look at some of the things that cause us to take years when we could have finished in less time. If we compare it to Israel exiting from Egypt the mindset of the people was slavery due to hundreds of years. This had gone on for some generations and was deeply embedded in them. Although they cried and prayed to Yahweh

Table of Contents

The Enemy Within

1. Introduction
2. Anger
3. Low Self-Esteem
4. Procrastination
5. Self-Doubt
6. Trust issues
7. Fear of Failure
8. Fear of Success
9. The Final Frontier

INTRODUCTION

In life we are exposed to many things from childhood on up. These experiences leave impressions on our minds and create strongholds that sometimes takes us years to get free from. Bondage and oppression can come in many forms. Some forms are physical like, illnesses brought on by how we think because of these life experiences. Some are mental but are just as bad as physical bondage. In this book we will look at some of the things that cause us to take years when we could have finished in less time. If we compare it to Israel exiting from Egypt the mindset of the people was slavery due to hundreds of years. This had gone on for some generations and was deeply embedded in them. Although they cried and prayed to Yahweh to be free, it came in physical form, but their minds took longer. When they left, they had some practices that they took from the Egyptians with other gods that Yahweh didn't like so much so that God literally let them walk through the wilderness for years instead of days so that a generation could die out. My hope is that after we review a few areas you will see something that will help you get free.

CHAPTER 1

The first area that I would like to discuss is "anger" because this one gets a lot of us in trouble. It is the root of a lot of situations simply because someone became angry and this led to other things which we will discuss further.

Anger

10. a strong feeling of displeasure and belligerence aroused by a wrong; wrath; ire.
11. *Chiefly British Dialect* . pain or smart, as of a sore.
12. *Obsolete* . grief; trouble.

Anger displaced can cause many problems. Based on the word we are to be slow to anger. There are instances in the word where we are told to turn the other cheek when someone does something to us that would invoke anger and cause us to sin. If we aren't careful, anger can cause us to do what Moses did and murder someone. In an instance when we lose control of our emotions we are put in a place where we are open to do something that we will regret, but because of an in the heat of the moment decision. Anger can cause you to alienate people since one of the coping mechanisms is to stop communicating. There were times I would be so angry with my husband that I would not talk to him for a week at a time, and we would be in the same space for hours.

Some have been pushed to a point of no return and committed an act that they now go to prison for.

Anger/rage are rooted in the spirit of jealously.

Spirits congregate or come in groupings.

-Murder - the unlawful premeditated killing of one human being by another. kill (someone) unlawfully and with premeditation.

-Revenge -Spite the action of inflicting hurt or harm on someone for an injury or wrong suffered at their hands.

-Jealousy - the state or feeling of being jealous.

-Cruelty - callous indifference to or pleasure in causing pain and suffering.

-Extreme competition - an event or contest in which people compete.

-Cause divisions - the action of separating something into parts or the process of being separated.

-Strife - angry or bitter disagreement over fundamental issues; conflict.

-Hatred - intense dislike or ill will.

-Contention - heated disagreement.

-Envy - a feeling of discontented or resentful longing aroused by someone else's possessions, qualities, or luck.

Anger is defined as a strong feeling of annoyance, displeasure, or hostility.

Ps 37:8 Stop being angry, put aside rage, and don't be upset — it leads to evil.

Prov 6:34 For jealousy drives a man into a rage; he will show no mercy when he takes revenge;

Prov 14:17, 29 He who is quick-tempered does stupid things, and one who does vile things is hated. Being slow to anger goes with great understanding, being quick-tempered makes folly still worse.

Prov 15:1 A gentle response deflects fury, but a harsh word makes tempers rise

Prov 16:32 He who controls his temper is better than a war hero, he who rules his spirit better than he who captures a city.

Prov 22:24 Don't associate with an angry man; make no hot-tempered man your companion.

Eccl 7:9 Don't be quick to get angry for [only] fools nurse anger.

Matt 5:22 [22] But I tell you that anyone who nurses anger against his brother will be subject to judgment; that whoever calls his brother, 'You good-for-nothing!' will be brought before the *Sanhedrin*; that whoever says, 'Fool!' incurs the penalty of burning in the fire of Gei-Hinnom!

Jas 1:19 [19] Therefore, my dear brothers, let every person be quick to listen but slow to speak, slow to get angry;

Love is going to be the way you combat anger. Self-control will be a way of balancing out anger. If you can get an individual to love themselves, their neighbor and their enemy they stand a strong chance of overcoming anger issues.

Prayer as an individual along with forgiveness will help bring about deliverance. This will be more of a private deliverance.

In a service setting, commands may be used to call out anger and the group of spirits that come with it. As I write this book, instances of anger and hatred appear in the lives of my friends. When you have your own flesh and blood tell you they hate you, and they disown you, then that is deep rooted hurt and anger. The person that is meant to hurt from it is devastated. The person full of anger can't see anything but the wrong that they feel was done to them. What I advised to the person on the receiving end was to forgive them and give them space and time. Everyone will have to heal from this, but then when the time is right showing the love of Adonai. Love is what it will take to combat anger as we know it covers a multitude of sins.

There are times as a kid and even an adult I would become so angry that my whole body would heat up. I would literally feel as though I was on fire. If you are not careful this can turn into rage and we all know rage is dangerous. Many people are in jail today because of the results of an action that came from rage. People have actually killed someone in a fit of rage. Some don't even remember as though they have blacked out or separated in their mind. Some kind of broke from reality. Some of the ways of dealing with anger is understanding your triggers. What is your way of escape, if you will? Some need to talk right away to get it out. Others need to write it out on paper. Whatever your release mechanism is make sure its non-violent. In elementary school on the bus ride from school, I had taken all I was going to take from this individual: When she said one more thing, I took her by the hair and slammed her head into the windows. It was only by the grace of God that it wasn't real glass, but more like plexi-glass. If I had just dealt with her when the issue originally started, I would have not let the anger build up to where I felt my only recourse was to try to hurt her. Communication is key to anything, but for people who struggle to manage anger it's vital since they have to release it or else explode. Some have attended anger management classes because they were locked up for a domestic violence dispute. One in particular told me that even though he did not want to go in the beginning that he was actually glad he went because he learned a lot. We may go in with one attitude and mindset, but when it's all over it's something that can help us overcome the struggle. When anger manifests there are many signs like skin color change, facial expressions change, blood pressure, may go up, and many other things.

Anger is tied to stress. When you become stressed you are more easily angered. With these two together in action you will find that its harder to manage. When we are under a lot of stress, we can perceive a situation as more threatening than it really is. This will trigger anger more quickly. Coping is something that may not get done when we are put in a fight or flight position. Based on your emotional response there can be an effect in the body which triggers a quick temper. If anger is not managed along with stress it can have a horrible effect on the body. If a anger is not managed along with stress, it can have a horrible effect on the body. Anger displaced can cause breathing, heart and other health issues. As I explain to people all the time you have to have some type of outlet. There has to be a way that you calm your body all the way down. Some of us pray, change what we are thinking about, exercise, take walks, etc. The first line of defense is to recognize your triggers and ensuring there is something in place to help you to remove yourself or cope. No one wants to be recognized as "The Incredible Hulk" because of the mental and physical damage.

CHAPTER 2

Low Self-Esteem

Some people are beautiful physically and personally, but in their mind they are ugly. They believe other people see them as ugly. Most often this will stem from a childhood traumatic event. Sometimes it's because someone over emphasized the importance of their outward appearance. Some may not have been very attractive as a kid and was teased so they became very sensitive and self-conscious. The same applies for the level of intelligence that someone has and how they feel they measure up or don't.

Anything that is related to you as a person from appearance, to talent, etc.

Meaning of Low Self-Esteem - **Low self-esteem** is characterized by a lack of confidence and feeling badly about oneself. People with **low self-esteem** often feel unlovable, awkward, or incompetent. ... "As observers of our own behavior, thoughts, and feelings, we not only register these phenomena in consciousness but also pass judgement on them.

Low self-esteem and quality of life. A low self-esteem can reduce the quality of a person's life in many different ways, including: Negative feelings – the constant self-criticism can lead to **persistent** feelings of sadness, **depression**, **anxiety**, anger, shame or guilt.

Signs of Low Self-Esteem

- Sensitivity to criticism.
- Social withdrawal.
- Hostility.
- Excessive preoccupation with personal problems.
- Physical symptoms such as fatigue, insomnia and headaches.

Causes of **low self-esteem**. Some of the many **causes** of **low self-esteem** may include: Unhappy childhood where parents (or other significant people such as teachers) were extremely critical. Poor academic performance in school resulting in a lack of **confidence**.

In my opinion low self-esteem can be tied to the spirit of heaviness. With that comes these other spirits.

- Excessive Mourning
- Sorrow Grief
- Broken-heart
- Suicidal thoughts
- Inner hurts - torn spirits
- Despair dejection
- Self-pity
- Insomnia
- Rejection
- Depression
- Heaviness

Many times, it will come out in conversation when you hear someone constantly go back to a topic. For instance, they may feel that many people don't like them. So, no matter what the topic is it will always end with "that's why people do xyz because they don't like me". Some will feel like someone is always out to control them. The same thing will happen with the conversation. It will go from a basic explanation of events to this person wants to control me. Not everyone is looking to do that. But because people crossed the line in the past and that place was never healed it operates like a broken record. When the needle of the record player gets to that scratch it will either skip or go on repeat.

Low self-esteem can cause you to miss out on so many opportunities. If you have always had dreams of being married but time seems to be moving extremely slow. You see many other people getting married, having kids, buying homes, etc. The enemy is in your ear saying you will never get married for one reason or another. A man comes along and even though he's no good for you due to self-esteem issues, the enemy has you accept him as is. You get married, have a child, and things go south quickly. You lose everything including your mind and almost your life. You are so used to abuse from your childhood that this level of dysfunction is something you are willing to accept because remember who else will marry me (my past, my weight, the number of children I have, etc.). Now you have added more years where your self-esteem is taking a beating and the damage is so instance, they may feel that many people don't like them. So, no matter what the topic is it will always end with "that's why people do xyz because they don't like me". Some will feel like someone is always out to control them. The same thing will happen with the conversation. It will go from a basic explanation of events to this person wants to control me. Not everyone is looking to do that. But because people crossed the line in the past and that place was never healed it operates like a broken record. When the needle of the record player gets to that scratch it will either skip or go on repeat.

Low self-esteem can cause you to miss out on so many opportunities. If you have always had dreams of being married but time seems to be moving extremely slow. You see many other people getting married, having kids, buying homes, etc. The enemy is in your ear saying you will never get married for one reason or another. A man comes along and even though he's no good for you due to self-esteem issues, the enemy has you accept him as is. You get married, have a child, and things go south quickly. You lose everything including your mind and almost your life. You are so used to abuse from your childhood that this level of dysfunction is something you are willing to accept because remember who else will marry me (my past, my weight, the number of children I have, etc.). Now you have added more years where your self-esteem is taking a beating and the damage is so bad that it spins you into an even deeper level of low self-esteem.

Low self-esteem can literally rob you of a full life. Your mind can literally bind you up so badly that you will live in a very small world. Your thoughts can literally imprison you. If you allow someone's opinion or something about yourself to hold you so captive then you have allowed low self-esteem to steal some of the happiest and fulfilled moments. For instance, some will go on vacation to a really warm climate and never wear a bathing suit to the beach because of religious reasons, or they don't like the way their body looks. Sometimes society ads and fads can make us feel less than what we are worth.

The pressure of this alone has driven some to deep depression. Others have gone the way of suicide. Then others have simply missed opportunities and open doors because they told themselves they weren't good enough. The way to review ourselves to make sure we haven't fallen prey to this is to examine our thoughts to see how we view ourselves and look at what impact those thoughts have. If they propel us forward then great'. If they don't then we have to begin to decree, declare and think another way. One of the best things you can do is to see yourself as God sees you. Once you do that it brings everything else into focus.

You know you are a procrastinator when you get invited to an event and your invitation has an earlier time than everyone else's. When you work with a procrastinator you will need a lot of patience. You may give them a chance to set a time to be ready for an event. They agree and you come to pick them up but to "no" surprise they are not ready. They have their hair rolled up, their clothes need to be ironed, and they have to get a shower. You ask yourself didn't we have a conversation about time and when to be ready? For someone who likes to be on time this doesn't work. The best thing you can do is leave them and see them when they get to the event. For some that sounds harsh, but when this has gone on for years you have to draw the line somewhere.

This was just an example using an event as the base. Just imagine procrastinating on the things of Christ. The downstream effect of not doing what Yahweh directs you to do when he tells you to do it can be detrimental. The great thing is that Adonai will send another because he cannot lie so his word has come to pass. Some drag their feet out of fear, some out of lack of confidence, and others its purely rebellion.

Procrastination can actually kill dreams. You can put something off so long that you actually could lose the desire to do it or the confidence to do it. These people have a tendency to be full of excuses. Some times its "those people" or "them" that has caused them not to move ahead because it won't be successful anyway. When you hesitate, you leave the door open for the enemy to deter and shift you from your destination.

3/25/11 Psychology Today

So, what causes people to really procrastinate outside of the reasons we talked about earlier? Sometimes it's a fear of failure. While others fear success. As crazy as it sounds most people fall in one category or another.

Scriptures about Procrastination

Proverbs 27:1 Don't boast about tomorrow, for you don't know what the day may bring.

Matthew 25:2 - 10 [2] Five of them were foolish and five were sensible. [3] The foolish ones took lamps with them but no oil, [4] whereas the others took flasks of oil with their lamps. [5] Now the bridegroom was late, so they all went to sleep. [6] It was the middle of the night when the cry rang out, 'The bridegroom is here! Go out to meet him!' ⁷ The girls all woke up and prepared their lamps for lighting. ⁸ The foolish ones said to the sensible ones, 'Give us some of your oil, because our lamps are going out.' ⁹ 'No,' they replied, 'there may not be enough for both you and us. Go to the oil dealers and buy some for yourselves.' ¹⁰ But as they were going off to buy, the bridegroom came. Those who were ready went with him to the wedding feast, and the door was shut.

Hebrews 3:7-19 ⁷ Therefore, as the *Ruach HaKodesh* says, "Today, if you hear God's voice, 8 don't harden your hearts, as you did in the Bitter Quarrel on that day in the Wilderness when you put God to the test.
9 Yes, your fathers put me to the test; they challenged me, and they saw my work for forty years!
10 Therefore, I was disgusted with that generation — I said, 'Their hearts are always going astray, they have not understood how I do things';
11 in my anger, I swore that they would not enter my rest."[a]

¹² Watch out, brothers, so that there will not be in any one of you an evil heart lacking trust, which could lead you to apostatize from the living God! ¹³ Instead, keep exhorting each other every day, as long as it is called **Today**, so that none of you will become

hardened by the deceit of sin. **14** For we have become sharers in the Messiah, provided, however, that we hold firmly to the conviction we began with, right through until the goal is reached.

15 Now where it says,

**"Today, if you hear God's voice,
don't harden your hearts, as you did in the Bitter Quarrel,"**
[b]

16 who were the people who, after they **heard, quarrel**ed so **bitter**ly? All those whom Moshe brought out of Egypt. **17** And with whom was God **disgusted for forty years**? Those who sinned — yes, they fell dead in the **Wilderness**! **18** And to whom was it that he **swore that they would not enter** his **rest**? Those who were disobedient. **19** So we see that they were unable to **enter** because of lack of trust.

Ezekiel 12:22-28 **22** "Human being, don't you have this proverb in the land of Isra'el, 'Time keeps passing, and none of the visions are fulfilled'? **23** Therefore tell them that *Adonai ELOHIM* says, 'I will put an end to that proverb; never again will they use it as a proverb in Isra'el.' Tell them, 'The time has come for the fulfillment of every vision. **24** There will no longer be empty visions or falsely optimistic divinations in the house of Isra'el, **25** because I am *ADONAI*. I will speak; and whatever statement I make, it will be accomplished. It will no longer be delayed; for in your days, your rebellious house, I will speak the word and accomplish it,' says *Adonai ELOHIM*."

26 Again, the word of *ADONAI* came to me: **27** "Human being, look! People from the house of Isra'el are saying, 'The vision he sees concerns the distant future; he is prophesying about a time far off.' **28** Therefore, say to them that *Adonai ELOHIM* says, 'None of my words will be delayed any more, but the word that I speak will be accomplished,' says *Adonai ELOHIM*."

In the word these scriptures deal with different types of procrastination. There were delays on both sides. Sometimes it seems as though Yeshua procrastinated but he didn't. He came right on time. He came when it was time.

CHAPTER 4

Self-Doubt

Spirits that often accompany self-doubt

- Spirit of Fear
- Ears / Phobias
- Torment - Horror
- Heart Attacks
- Fear of Man
- Nightmares Terrors
- Fear of Death
- Anxiety - Stress
- Untrusting - Doubt

Definition of Self-Doubt - lack of confidence in the reliability of one's own motives, personality, thought, etc.

There are times when the Lord gives you a word about what he called you to do? He may show you things that you will do under his direction and power. But now self-doubt will come in and say you didn't see what you saw. Simply that you could not possibly accomplish that.

An example is if you have been running a business for 20 or more years, and you decide you want to expand, but constantly talk yourself out of it. You have the history, a successful track record and the resources to do it, but yet and still you hold. You talk to so many people and get some many other opinions, and you say because of the opposition you are not moving forward quickly. With all of the success that you have had you doubt that you can make it at the next level because of people. Before you know it you have allowed self-doubt to keep you in the same position for another 10 or 15 years, and the amount of success that you could have experienced you will never see.

Now bullying has become a huge deal. You can doubt yourself to the point of being unproductive in life because you have allowed someone in life to over shadow you to the point where you doubt things you know you can do. Don't allow the enemy to push you to a point of doubting yourself to that degree. In the Bible the disciples doubted that Yashua cared for them by making sure they woke him in the boat because of the storm. Yeshua was annoyed by the lack of faith, doubt, and rebuked the wind and the rain? The thing about this is they had seen him do so many miracles before, but still they doubted. This can cripple you to the point where you don't move out on things you should. If Yahweh was to tell you something you would doubt it because trouble came to the point that you doubted the power of God.

CHAPTER 5

Trust Issues

> Definition of Trust - reliance on the integrity, strength, ability, surety, etc., of a person or thing; confidence.
>
> - confident expectation of something; hope.
> - confidence in the certainty of future payment for property or goods received; credit:

For some trust was broken at a very young age. Some were so young that it was their parents that neglected something meaningful which left them vulnerable and exposed. As a young kid the expectation is that the parents would protect. While in many cases that did not happen so children did not happen. So, children developed either deep rooted emotional issues or other coping mechanisms. These things turn into major problems later. If a person never heals from this, they can often see everyone and every situation as untrustworthy. These thoughts can make someone seem paranoid and delusional. Once trust has been broken it's not easily regained. Often times married couples will betray each other's trust and some of the main areas are money and extra relationships. For some, they are able to forgive and move on. Others, every time an argument happens about anything else, they bring up the same incident that caused the distrust. So unfortunately, it has become a seed of unforgiveness and bitterness. When people constantly tell you that they are going to do something, and they never follow through, it will cause you to distrust everything they say. It's better to under promise and over deliver and at least you would have fulfilled your word and exceeded a person's expectations. Often times we are asked to trust the Lord in places we cannot see or refuse to believe in. If you are struggling trusting in man whom, you can see, imagine how hard it can be to trust a God you cannot see. Trust issues can cause you to miss out on someone who was really sent to bless you. There is a gentleman that I know who always had a lot of women so when it came time for him to be married, he stayed so suspicious because of his past behavior that it did not last. If you know that you've done a lot you cannot cast that on someone else. If they are at the store too long, or if you think someone is in the background while they are on the phone, etc. You can literally drive someone away from you and out of your life. It all stems from you knowing the untrustworthy things you did and believing that everyone is just like you. We really have to examine why we are so suspect and get to the root of the problem. If we don't, a good portion of our life can be lived in a reality that only exists in your head. Wouldn't it be better trusting Adonai and allowing the Ruach Hakadesh to lead you and guide you in to all truth. Understand that people will lie and mislead and betray your trust, but it's how you deal with it which makes the difference.

While married my trust was broken and it took a really long time to heal. I trusted my husband immensely, but that was taken for granted and tossed in the wind. His infidelity was hard to swallow because of all that was done. One day I came home from work, and my husband said you have 60 days to find another place to live. I'm moving without you somewhere else. I managed to do that thinking ok at some point we will work this out and figure out how to move on from here. One whole year went by and we did not, as a matter of fact it got worse. At the end of the one year he called to say that he had an extra marital affair. This affair was with a co-worker that ended very badly. He wanted to make amends to see if we could salvage our relationship. For me, it was hard for me to trust as I had in the past, so my answer was no.

CHAPTER 6

Fear of Failure

1. **Definition of Failure** - lack of success. "an economic policy that is doomed to failure"
2. the omission of expected or required action. "their failure to comply with the basic rules"

I own a business called "Professional Administrative Services, LLC". In this business I assist small business owners with all kinds of administrative tasks. For those looking to start a business I usually consult with them and go over what it will take to get started from a paperwork standpoint (choosing a name, licensing, business type, etc.) This group of people have the hardest time because they haven't started the business. They feel they have a great idea and want to move forward but defeating thoughts often keep them from doing just that. After they develop their business plan which gives them a road map on what it's going to take financially to run the business most people stop right there. They wonder how they will be able to maintain the bills they have as well as take on the debt of a business. Most will place that business plan on the shelf and never pick it back up again. Others will make several attempts but still won't follow through to get the business up and off the ground. The fear of failure paralyzes some folks to the point that they never even allow themselves to experience success.

What most people know, but don't often have enough courage to walk out, is an actual failure. When you speak with business owners who have been up and running for years, they will tell you about their failures. They will in fact talk about times when they almost walked away from the business completely. But yet in still they kept moving forward and have become the successful person you see today. Failures often help us grow. They are valuable lessons that most of the time you only need to learn once. Some business owners have failed several times and lost thousands of dollars but they still started over. This is just one example of an area of failure but you can apply this to anything (public speaking, athletics, writing a book, etc.).

Faith is going to be your biggest weapon against fear. You will have to trust in areas that you cannot see. You will have to step out on things that don't seem to be stable. We are expected to have faith at least the size of a mustard seed. If you have seen an actual mustard see that's pretty small.

CHAPTER 7

Fear of Success

- a distressing emotion aroused by impending danger, evil, pain, etc., whether the threat is real or imagined; the feeling or condition of being afraid.
- a specific instance of or propensity for such a feeling: an abnormal fear of heights.
- concern or anxiety; solicitude:

It sounds crazy but there are people who are literally afraid of success. Some people sabotage their own things whether it's conscious or subconscious. Fear can cause us to do some crazy things. I'm reminded of a short saying that described how a person was gripping the end of a rope terrified to let go because they thought they would plunge to their death. Since their eyes were tightly shut, they could not see that if they let go their feet would touch the ground. This is how close some people are to success. Since fear has them gripped, they never move past the initial phase. Success scares some people because they feel it will obligate them to give more than what they can. Some have built up a paranoia around people and believe that people are trying to kill them for their money so they would rather stay at moderate pay or be inconspicuous.

Some would rather just fit in instead of rising to the top. Can you imagine having the ability to win a race but you slow down just so others could pass you by? As off as that sounds this is essentially what happens when someone chooses not to succeed out of fear. In 2 Timothy 1:7 states "For God gave us a Spirit who produces not timidity, but power, love and self-discipline". If he gave us a spirit that doesn't produce timidity than anything else, we should be rejecting. Trust in Adonai with all your heart and know that the Ruach Hakodesh will lead and guide you into all truth. You can be successful and not fear people, but enjoy it and bless people with the abundance that you have been given through your success.

CHAPTER 8

The Final Frontier

The mind is truly a place where many battles are fought. Set yourself up to win over the struggles in your mind. If you battle with depression put on the garment of praise. If you are a procrastinator, set your clock a whole hour early. If you are fearful of succeeding, walk out an invention, business idea, or goal and enjoy the success. In order to win the battle with the enemy within you have to push past what keeps you hostage. Yahweh has spoken of promises concerning you and the only one who can keep you from some of them is you. Think through times where you have allowed the enemy in your mind to win. We are emotional beings, often times they coupled with how we think can get us completely off track. Let's take a closer look at the brain and how emotions affect the brain.

1. Happiness activates several areas of the brain, including the right frontal cortex, the precuneus, the left amygdala, and the left insula. This activity involves connections between awareness (frontal cortex and insula) and the "feeling center" (amygdala) of the brain.

2. Fear activates the bilateral amygdala, the hypothalamus and areas of the left frontal cortex. This involves some thinking (frontal cortex), a "gut" feeling (amygdala), and a sense of urgency typically associated with survival (the hypothalamus.)

3. Sadness is associated with increased activity of the right occipital lobe, the left insula, the left thalamus the amygdala and the hippocampus. The hippocampus is strongly linked with memory, and it makes sense that awareness of certain memories is associated with feeling sad.

Sadness has been studied more than the other emotions because depression may last for a long time; the effects of antidepressants can be measured based on improved symptoms.

4. Disgust is an interesting feeling that is often associated with avoidance. This emotion that is associated with activation and connections between the left amygdala, the left inferior frontal cortex, and the insular cortex.

5. Anger is an important emotion that many people, adults and children alike, try to control. Anger is associated with activation of the right hippocampus, the amygdala, both sides of the prefrontal cortex and the insular cortex.

6. Surprise is an emotion that can either make you feel good or it can make you feel bad. Surprise activates the bilateral inferior frontal gyrus and the bilateral hippocampus. The hippocampus is strongly associated with memory, and the element of surprise is, by nature, associated with experiencing something that you do not remember or do not expect.

Source: https://www.neurologytimes.com/blog/how-brain-processes-emotions

In the end, make the decision to move past your emotions and defeating thoughts. You will experience great levels of accomplishments and success.

References

Unless otherwise indicated, all Scripture quotations in this study are from The Complete Jewish Bible.

Chapter 1: Anger .... Pg. 36 Strongman's His Name What's His Game?

Chapter 2: Low Self-Esteem ... Pg. 64 Strongman's His Name What's His Game?

Chapter 4: Self-Doubt - Pg. 110 Strongman's His Name What's His Game?

Chapter 8: The Final Frontier ..

https://www.neurologytimes.com/blog/how-brain-processes-emotions

About the Author

Prophetess Deirdre Avant called, appointed, and anointed by God as a prophetess to the nations. She is the founder and president of a ministry named *Tefillah*. In order for her to be here, God allowed her to be born through Robert Green and Viola Woolford. This was always in the mind and the plan of God that He would order this woman of God's steps regarding ministry. She was called into the prophetic office in the summer of 2002 and acknowledged her calling in the fall of 2002. Prophetess Deirdre Avant was properly birthed into the office and given impartation by her prophetic father, Prophet Raymond P. Stansbury of Wilmington, DE. Pastor of "Prophetic House of Truth Outreach" on Friday, May 14, 2003. She has attended an intense six-month course at The P.I.T. School of Ministry in 2003. God confirmed her calling into the office through dreams and visions. After the confirmation of her calling she did the necessary things to enhance the prophetic that was in her. The devil thought that fornication and rebellion would have kept the mouth of this prophetess closed; even though that weapon was formed it did not come against her.

Gifted in administration and an accomplished coordinator, she is the CEO of Professional Administrative Services and the founder of Daughters of Zion, Inc. – a non-profit organization that ministers to young women dealing with foster care. She is a covenant member and Licensed Minister of *New Destiny Fellowship, Wilmington, DE*, under the covering of Bishop *Thomas Wesley Weeks, Sr.* where she functions as Intercessor, Altar Worker and Ministry Administrator.

Hobbies and Talents: She has operated in music ministry over the years between the Delaware, Maryland, and Virginia Area. She also enjoys volunteer work with children who have learning disabilities. It is Prophetess Avant's purpose to speak the true word of God, *which* will destroy the works of the devil. She is a single mom to Brandon and Arion. Her Pastoral father was the late Rev. Mack; her spiritual Mothers are Pastor

Ward, Ms. Carolyn Graham, and Pastor Gamble.

What she really wants you to know is that she is a no-nonsense type of person. She wants people to be real with her. Lies and deceit are of the devil and they need to be put to rest. She is a woman of the truth and has no problems with standing up for the truth regardless of who is telling the lie.

www.ingramcontent.com/pod-product-compliance
Lightning Source LLC
Chambersburg PA
CBHW051717040426
42446CB00008B/925